GW00657894

East End Eats

Published by Clink Street Publishing 2023
Copyright © 2023

First edition.

The author asserts the moral right under the Copyright, Designs and Patents Act 1988 to be identified as the author of this work.

All rights reserved. No part of this publication may be reproduced, stored in a retrieval system or transmitted, in any form or by any means without the prior consent of the author, nor be otherwise circulated in any form of binding or cover other than that with which it is published and without a similar condition being imposed on the subsequent purchaser.

ISBN:
978-1-912850-16-7 - hardback
978-1-912850-17-4 - ebook

For Jean

Contents

~~~~

East End Eats

Recipes from East London's coolest restaurants, bars, cafes and market stalls

STEPHAN BUCHER

Introduction

I first had the idea for *East End Eats* at home in spring of 2017. I had lost my wallet on the previous bank holiday Monday and had to cancel my trip to Australia because I had no credit cards, driver's licence, or way of paying for anything during my trip. I stayed at home in London for days looking out the window wondering; could I holiday in my very own suburb?

The idea for *East End Eats* was never about beginning at the high end. It was about making a book that would suit both a Londoner and a visitor. In the ten years that I have lived in London, Shoreditch and the East End has seen massive regeneration, transforming from a no-go area with high crime rates, to a place populated by creative types and artists. It's now one of the most desirable places to live in London, if not the world.

The East End has gone from strength to strength and despite the duality between the original inhabitants, to the mix of city bankers who work just down the street, there is an unusual harmony in the area and that is something quite unique to London.

The people in the area at the weekend differ to those who are here midweek. Weekend markets like Brick Lane, Columbia Road and Broadway Market are full of both visitors and Londoners; however take a walk along Regent's Canal on a Tuesday afternoon and you will see locals walking their dogs, cycling and generally doing outdoors exercise.

In this digital age, we all rely on our phones to hunt for the coolest places to go, but sometimes we just need to sit down and relax with a book that is both beautiful and evocative – there's nothing that can be compared to the tactile nature of turning a page and being inspired by the images and the narrative that has been written about a certain area. So with this book, that concept is in your hands! Go ahead and explore the East End of London: It's my home – it could be your home one day too – but at least you can explore like a local.

A huge thank you must go to the restauranteurs, chefs, owners and PR agents for their amazing support over the years in compiling this book. The Covid pandemic in 2020 through 2022 took its toll on the dining and nightlife industry – not all establishments made it through, but their recipes live on.

Cheers
Stephan

Early Bird

Breakfast and brunch

~~~~~~~~~~~~~~~~~~~~~~

The Bach Hoxton
"Sweet As" Corn Fritters – Gluten-Free

The Bach Broadway
Decadent Gluten-Free Chocolate Brownie

SHED
The Perfect Flat White

Galvin La Chapelle
Apple Tarte Tatin with Crème Normande

Blixen
Chocolate Fondant, Coconut Sorbet (vegan)

The Bach Hoxton

"Sweet As" Corn fritters – Gluten-Free

I love The Bach. It feels like a home away from home. A Bach (pronounced 'batch') is a small, often very modest holiday home or beach house. Baches are an iconic part of New Zealand history and culture and are great places to unwind.

Bach Hoxton is a bustling East London weekend brunch destination on Hoxton Street. They relentlessly bang out awesome Allpress Coffee alongside all-day brunches and lunches; all served with friendly Kiwi hospitality. Both of their venues have a great vibe, so drop by and check them out.

SERVES 6

- 550g sweetcorn
- 360g Greek yogurt
- 4 large free-range eggs
- 160g polenta
- 100g gluten-free self-raising flour
- 15gm bicarbonate soda
- 6 spring onions chopped
- Coriander bunch chopped
- Salt and pepper to taste
- Olive oil for frying

To Serve:
- 3 avocados, halved and sliced
- 6 rashers of bacon, fried
- 250g Halloumi cheese, sliced and grilled
- 1 cup of chilli jam
- ½ cup of aioli

Add the Greek yoghurt and eggs to a large bowl and mix well.

Once combined, add the sweetcorn, polenta, flour and bicarbonate soda and mix until combined into a lumpy batter.

Heat olive oil in a non-stick frying pan. Use a large ladel or spoon to add the batter to the pan. Each fritter should be about 2 inches across.

Cook the fritters for about 2 minutes until golden brown on one site before turning them to finish cooking on the other side.

Keep the fritters warm in a low over while you cook the others in batches.

To serve, place three fritters on a warm plate. Top with the sliced avocado, a rasher of bacon and the halloumi cheese. Drizzle each serving with a tablespoon of chilli jam and a dollop of aioli.

Perfect drink match:
a chilled glass of prosecco

15

The second of The Bach's East London outposts is located on Broadway Market. All their food is produced from carefully sourced ingredients – local where possible. Their ethos is interesting: they tightly control the kitchens their food is produced in and are able to cater for to a variety of dietary requirements like gluten-free, coeliac, vegan and lactose-free. As well as brunches and lunches, they have amazing fresh smoothies and juices and their house-made gluten-free cakes, sweets and takeaway lunches are outstanding.

Also, check out their Bach loyalty scheme giving you 10 percent credit back to spend on your next visit – it won't take long for you to quickly get addicted to The Bach brunch and coffee fix. They also stock a nicely edited retail range including a gluten-free granola which has won a Taste Award. Come on a weekend and you can even choose a cake from their cake tower after you've ordered a brunch to set you right for the weekend, of course!

- *250g unsalted butter*
- *350g caster sugar*
- *230g dark chocolate buttons*
- *6 medium free-range eggs*
- *200g gluten-free plain flour*
- *70g cocoa powder*
- *Large pinch of salt*

....

Preheat the oven to 180 Celsius.

Mix sugar and eggs in an electric mixer on a high speed until the mixture goes pale.

Melt butter in a large pan on a low heat. Add the chocolate buttons until melted ensuring it doesn't overcook or burn on the bottom of the pan, as this will ruin the taste.

Sieve the gluten-free flour and the cocoa powder into a bowl.

Add the melted chocolate and butter mixture to the eggs and sugar. On a slow mixing speed add the flour and cocoa mix one spoonful at a time.

Spray a large baking tray with cooking spray and line with greaseproof paper, cutting into the corners and removing the excess.

Pour the mixture into the tray and ensure it is spread evenly.

Place into the preheated over and cook for 18 minutes. The brownie should still have a wobble when removed from the oven and must be cooled before slicing and serving.

Perfect drink match:
oat-milk flat white

I just love SHED. It's been a firm fixture on the East London coffee scene for years now. Their two Haggerston sites are slightly different. The one closet to the Haggerston Overground offers amazing coffee, pastries and a wine shop. While the one around the corner on Kingsland Road is more of a deli with artisanal produce and provisions – I visit more than once a week to get wonderful hard-to-source ingredients.

- *18g ground espresso, or 1 espresso pod*
- *100ml milk of your choice*

You will also need
- *the right cup , 150-200ml capacity*

....

Make around 35ml espresso using your coffee machine and pour into the base of your cup.

Steam your milk so that it has around 1-2cm of foam on top.

Hold the jug so that the spout is about 3-4cm above the cup and pour the milk in steadily.

As the volume within the cup increases, bring the jug as close to the surface of the drink as possible whilst aiming to pour into the centre.

Once the milk jug is almost touching the surface of the coffee, tilt the jug to speed up the rate of pour.

As you accelerate, the milk will hit the back of the cup and start naturally folding in on itself to create a pattern on the top.

Galvin la Chapelle
Apple Tarte Tatin with Crème Normande

If I want to impress someone, be they a visitor from out of town, or a loved one for any occasion really, I bring them here. The space itself is a triumph of blending the historic envelope of the building with contemporary and luxe design elements. I can't get enough of the place, but do make a reservation as its Michelin star makes it a sought-after table in London.

SERVES 4

- *120g Puff Pastry*
- *110g softened salted butter*
- *130g caster sugar*
- *7 Braeburn apples, peeled, halved and cored*

For the crème Normande:
- *120ml crème fraîche*
- *40g icing sugar*
- *1 ½ tablespoons*

....

Preheat the oven to 160C

Roll the puff pastry out on a lightly floured surface to a 21cm round. Prick all over with a fork and rest in the fridge for 40 minutes.

Spread the butter over the bottom of a 20cm tarte Tatin mould or an ovenproof, non-stick frying pan. Sprinkle the caster sugar over in an even layer, then arrange the apple halves over the sugar, standing them on their sides, with 2 halves in the middle.

Lay the pastry round over the apples, tucking the edges down the side. Place the mould or pan over a medium heat on the hob for about 10 minutes or until the sugar starts to caramelise.

Transfer it to the oven preheated to 160°C/Gas Mark 3 and bake for 1.5 hours.

For the crème Normande, mix all the ingredients together in a bowl, then cover with cling film and refrigerate for 1 hour.

Remove the tart from the oven and leave to cool for at least 30 minutes. Invert the tarte Tatin on to a chopping board and cut it into 4 portions.

Serve a generous spoonful of crème Normande with each portion of the warm tarte Tatin.

Blixen

Chocolate Fondant, Coconut Sorbet (vegan)

Blixen is located on the edge of the bustling and vibrant Old Spitalfields Market – a restaurant with its own peaceful atmosphere and vibe. Filled with plants and natural light aplenty, Blixen is an unexpected escape from the buzz of the city.

With a focus on casual European dining and beautiful design, we practise the true spirit of hospitality – arrive happy, leave happier.

We are open seven days a week, offering brunch, lunch and dinner, complemented by an eclectic wine list and exceptional cocktails – both upstairs and at Bar Three, our subterranean cocktail lounge.

So whether it's for brunch with the gang, a romantic dinner in the garden conservatory, or a prime position at the kitchen counter, there's a space at Blixen that will suit you.

Ganache:

- *70g dark chocolate*
- *45g almond milk*
- *10g sunflower spread*

Sponge:

- *40g gluten-free flour*
- *20g almond powder*
- *1 tsp gluten-free baking powder*
- *30g sugar*
- *70g almond milk*
- *10g sunflower spread*
- *10g cocoa powder*
- *pinch of salt*

Chocolate sauce:

- *750g dark chocolate*
- *100g sunflower spread*
- *900g almond milk*
- *Coconut sorbet:*
- *Sugar 420g*
- *Glucose 50g*
- *Water 280ml*
- *1 kg coconut puree*
- *Coconut crumb:*
- *100g sugar*
- *80g coconut flakes*

Start by prepping the sorbet. In a saucepan, boil the sugar, glucose and water until it has a consistency of syrup. Cool down, then add coconut puree and churn in an ice cream machine. It will need to rest few hours in the freezer before it can be used.

Next, make the coconut crumb by heating sugar in a saucepan, until obtaining a light brown caramel. Into this, incorporate coconut flakes and mix thoroughly. Cool it down on a sheet of baking paper, blend when cold and keep aside.

After, make the fondant. Start with the ganache by heating the chocolate, almond milk and sunflower spread in a bain-marie until all are totally dissolved.

Next, move on to the sponge. In a separate bowl, mix all the dry sponge ingredients and then add the almond milk and sunflower spread to make the cake.

Spray foil cups with some grease spray, put 4mm of cake dough on the bottom, 2 spoons of ganache in the middle, then cover with the remaining cake dough up to 5mm to the top.

Cook at 180C for 12 minutes.

While the cake bakes, mix all the ingredients for the chocolate sauce into a saucepan and bring to the boil.

Once cooked, take the fondant out of the mould and place in the centre of the plate. Spoon the chocolate sauce on top and finish with coconut crumbs and a scoop of sorbet.

Small Bites & Sides

Global tapas

~~~~~~~~~~

Sager + Wilde
The Ultimate Cheese Toastie

Poptata
GuacaFries

Poptata
*Sriracha Mayonnaise, Grilled Halloumi &
Smashed Avocado*

Mr White's English Chophouse
Dauphinoise Potatoes

Dirty Bones
Cheeseburger Dumplings

Sager + Wilde

This place is just a short walk from where I live in East London and it makes for the perfect pitstop if I'm coming home from the city. The space is casual and very much on trend with industrial touches – service is always on-point too and their wines are just a delight.

MAKES 1

- *Soft white sourdough slices – 2 per toastie*
- *Slices of Montgomery cheddar (from Neal's Yard)*
- *Spring onions or jalapeños finely chopped*
- *A knob of French butter*

·······································

This is a wonderfully simple recipe!

Butter the outside of each slice of bread with the French butter.

On the inside of the toastie, add the sliced cheese and the onions or jalapenos (or both).

Add the other slice of bread to make a sandwich.

In a medium to hot non-stick pan, gently cook on both side for about 6-7 min or until the cheese is melted or the sourdough is crispy and golden.

Setting up amidst the hustle and bustle of the other colourful food stalls, Marco and Luca (the minds behind Poptata) looked at each other and smiled, sensing that their idea really was going to fill an exciting niche.

It was the height of London's casual dining revolution, and the pair had the brainwave to forge a brilliantly simple new strand within an emerging street food scene – a space that was opening up genuinely good food-on-the-go to foodies bored with the rigidity of traditional restaurants.

With more than 14 years' experience in the luxury hospitality industry, Marco and Luca decided to go back to basics and came up with a plan to offer Londoners something familiar and comforting, yet done in a very different way. Taking one of the best loved beacons of British culinary tradition, the (Italian) pair stole a march on their homegrown rivals and decided to celebrate the humble chip. And Poptata was born, heralding the arrival of London's best-ever-snack-time-favourite – STREET FRIES!

MAKES 2 PORTIONS

- *1l sunflower oil*
- *200ml olive oil*
- *4 agria potatoes*
- *1 avocado*
- *halloumi*
- *Sriracha mayonnaise*
- *Herbal seasoning (rosemary, thyme, oregano, basil, garlic, black pepper)*
- *Salt*

Peel the potatoes and cut lengthways into roughly 1cm in slices. Cut each slice into fairly thick chips and rinse in a colander under plenty of cold water to remove excess starch. (If you have time, it's worth letting the chips soak in a bowl of cold water for several hours, or overnight.) Pat dry with kitchen paper.

Heat a deep, heavy-bottomed saucepan half-full of the sunflower oil to 130C. It's important to use a cooking thermometer and check the temperature regularly. Alternatively, use an electric deep-fat fryer heated to 130C.

Using a large, metal, slotted spoon, gently lower half the chips into the hot oil and stir carefully. Fry for 10 minutes, or until cooked through but not browned.

Remove the chips from the pan with a slotted spoon and set aside to drain on plenty of kitchen paper. Repeat the process with the remaining chips. (The chips can be left for several hours at this stage.)

When ready to serve, reheat the oil to 190C. With a slotted spoon, lower all the par-cooked chips gently into the pan and cook for 4-5 minutes, or until crisp and golden-brown. Remove from the pan with a slotted spoon and drain on kitchen paper.

To serve: Tip chips into a serving dish and sprinkle with the herbal seasoning and salt. Try Smashed Avocado, Grilled Halloumi and Sriracha Mayonnaise as an accompaniment

Perfect drink match:
Mi Hermosita (see page 59)

Poptata *Sriracha Mayonnaise, Grilled Halloumi & Smashed Avocado*

MAKES ENOUGH FOR 2 SERVINGS

Sriracha Mayonnaise:
- *¼ cup mayonnaise*
- *1 tbsp sriracha chilli sauce, or any preferred chili hot sauce*
- *2 tsp lime or lemon juice*
- *1tsp soy sauce (optional)*
- *salt to taste*

Grilled Halloumi:
- *225g Cypriot halloumi*
- *Extra virgin olive oil*

Smashed Avocado:
- *2 ripe avocadoes*
- *1 medium red chilli, sliced (seeds removed for a less spicy version)*
- *1 garlic clove, crushed*
- *2tsp lime juice*
- *Sea salt*
- *Extra virgin olive oil*

For the Sriracha Mayonnaise:

Add mayonnaise to a mixing bowl. Add the Sriracha chilli sauce and stir to combine. Pour in the lime or lemon juice and soy sauce.

Mix well to combine the flavours. Add salt to taste and serve.

For the Grilled Halloumi:

Preheat an outdoor grill or stove-top griddle pan over medium-high heat/ flame, about 180 Celsius.

Cut the halloumi into approximately half-centimetre slices.

Once hot, place the halloumi on the grill. Flip each slice after about 3 minutes, or once golden-brown grill marks appear.

Drizzle with extra virgin olive oil and serve.

For the Smashed Avocado:

Cut the avocadoes in half and remove the stones. Slice into segments and place the avocado in a bowl. Add the chilli, garlic, lime juice, a pinch of sale and a drizzle of extra virgin olive oil.

Mash with a fork to the desired consistency. It can be as chunky or smooth as you like.

Mr White's English Chophouse

Marco Pierre White has teamed-up with New Road Hotel to launch his first ever Chophouse in London. Mr. White's English Chophouse gives a nod to tradition and centres on everything that chophouses are famed for: meat and hearty portions.

The Chophouse menu cleverly combines English classics whilst also introducing a little French flair that epitomizes Marco's cooking style. The menu centres around steaks, grills and chops.

SERVES 4

- *420g thinly sliced potatoes*
- *200ml double cream*
- *1 garlic clove*
- *1g salt*
- *1g black pepper*
- *3g thyme*
- *30g Gruyere cheese*
- *70g Cheddar cheese*
- *3g rosemary*

In a pan add garlic, cream and herbs, bring to a simmer and leave for one hour, pass through a fine sieve and use for the below.

Preheat the oven to 185C.

Add one layer of potatoes to tray, cover the layer with the seasoned cream. Add another layer of potatoes to the tray, this time add Cheddar and Gruyere cheese mix to potatoes. Repeat this process alternating between cream and cheese until the tray is full.

Cover the top with aluminium foil and place in the oven to cook at 185C for approximately 45 minutes. Once cooked, remove foil to brown top, then chill and pre-portion prior to serving.

Dirty Bones is all about the good vibes and high fives – add a generous dose of NYC-inspired food and drink plus a seriously good soundtrack that people want to listen to while they eat, and you have the ultimate venue in which to drink and play.

Housed in an iconic Grade II-listed heritage building on Club Row, Dirty Bones' history-steeped restaurant and cocktail bar was once home to 1960s pub and institution Knave of Clubs, and they've kept the party alive today. I love Dirty Bones as the perfect post-work cocktail hang out, late-night drinking den or for dinner with friends. Signature dishes include NYC-inspired comfort food classics such as Chicken & Waffles, Flat Iron Steak and Cheeseburger Dumplings.

MAKES 20

- 250g mince beef
- 90g American cheese – roughly chopped
- 15g superfine capers – finely chopped
- 20g cornichons – finely diced
- 1 tsp sriracha
- 30g tomato ketchup
- 2 x tsp Dijon mustard
- Salt & pepper to taste
- 1 packet of gyoza skins
- Spring onions finely sliced
- Black & white sesame seeds

For the Burger Sauce:
- 70g French's Mustard
- 30g tomato ketchup

....

Add the mince, cheese, capers, gherkins, sriracha, tomato ketchup and Dijon mustard in a bowl, season with salt and pepper to taste and mix the ingredients together.

Press the mixture into 20 small oval-shaped patties weighing pprox.. 25 grams each.

Fill the gyoza skins with the mix and press the sides together, sealing the edge with water.

Pan fry five dumplings at a time in a little oil to colour the base.

Add 50ml of water and cover with a lid, steam until cooked.

For the dipping sauce, add the French's Mustard and tomato ketchup to a bowl and mix together.

Spoon the sauce into a small serving dish or ramekin to serve on side of plate.

Arrange dumplings on plate and garnish with spring onions and black & white sesame seeds.

Signatures

Main dishes

~~~

Galvin la Chapelle
Lasagne of Crab with Beurre Nantais

Mr White's English Chophouse
Duck Pie, Young Spinach and Chicken Jus

Mr White's English Chophouse
Roast Rump of Lamb Dijonnaise

Blixen
Cajun spiced monkfish, truffled couscous risotto, kale & red salsa

Angelina
Unagi Risotto

Galvin la Chapelle

Lasagne of Crab with Beurre Nantais

If I want to impress someone, be they a visitor from out of town, or a loved one for any occasion really, I bring them here. The space itself is a triumph of blending the historic envelope of the building with contemporary and luxe design elements. I can't get enough of the place, but do make a reservation as its Michelin star makes it a sought-after table in London.

SERVES 10

- *500g of pasta dough*

For the mousse:
- *400g fresh scallops (white part only)*
- *480ml double cream*
- *A pinch each of sea salt and cayenne pepper*
- *650g fresh white crab meat*

For the sauce:
- *1 shallot, finely diced*
- *200g unsalted butter, chilled and diced*
- *50ml white wine*
- *25ml white wine vinegar*
- *50ml water*
- *100ml chicken stock*
- *25ml double cream*
- *1 tablespoon finely chopped chives*
- *sea salt and freshly ground white pepper*

Roll the pasta out on a lightly floured surface until it is thin enough to go through the thickest setting on a pasta machine. Feed the dough through the machine, reducing the setting by one notch each time, until it is thin enough for you to see your fingers through it – this may well take 8–10 rolls through the machine. Cut the pasta sheets into manageable lengths, about 30cm. Blanch them separately in a large pan of boiling salted water for 1 minute, then plunge into iced water and leave for 1 minute. Drain in a colander and lay out on a work surface. Using a metal ring 6cm in diameter, cut out 30 rounds. Lay out on a baking tray covered with cling film and store in the fridge.

For the mousse, place the bowl of a food processor in the freezer for 1 hour so it is thoroughly chilled, then blitz the scallop flesh in it for 3–4 minutes, scraping down the sides with a plastic spatula 3 or 4 times, until thoroughly puréed. With the machine running, slowly add half the double cream. Season with salt and cayenne pepper, then add the remainder of the cream a little faster. Transfer the mixture to a bowl and fold in the white crab meat. Taste and adjust the seasoning. To assemble the lasagnes, place 1 disc of pasta in the bottom of each of 10 6cm metal rings, 4.5cm deep. Half fill each ring with some of the scallop and crab mixture, then add another pasta disc. Spoon some of the remaining scallop and crab mixture into each ring and then top with a final disc of pasta. Refrigerate the lasagnes while you make the sauce.

To make the sauce, cook the shallot in a little of the butter in a small pan until soft but not coloured. Add the white wine, vinegar and water and simmer until reduced to a thick, syrupy consistency. Add the chicken stock and boil until reduced by half, then add the double cream and boil for 1 minute. Whisk in the cold butter a little at a time, maintaining the heat in the sauce as you go. Adjust the seasoning and keep warm. Put the lasagnes in a steamer and cook for 12 minutes, then transfer each one to a serving bowl. Run a small knife around the inside of each metal ring and remove it. Add the chives to the sauce, spoon it over the lasagnes and serve.

Mr White's English Chophouse

Marco Pierre White has teamed-up with New Road Hotel to launch his first ever Chophouse in London. Mr. White's English Chophouse gives a nod to tradition and centres on everything that chophouses are famed for: meat and hearty portions.

The Chophouse menu cleverly combines English classics whilst also introducing a little French flair that epitomizes Marco's cooking style. The menu centres around steaks, grills and chops.

For the pie mix:
- *20g smoked turkey rashers*
- *20g minced turkey*
- *40g roasted duck meat*
- *1 egg, beaten*
- *10ml double cream*
- *3g pie seasoning (below)*
- *40g puff pastry*

Pie seasoning:
- *5g each of black peppercorns, coriander seeds, allspice, juniper berries, cloves, cumin seeds, yellow mustard powder and ground nutmeg*
- *4 bay leaves*
- *5g dried mushrooms*

To serve:
- *20g baby spinach, steamed and buttered*
- *25ml chicken jus*

Preheat the oven to 200C fan.

Blend the ingredients for the pie seasoning in a food processor to a fine texture.

In a food processor, chop the minced turkey, the turkey rashers, the duck meat, half the beaten egg, the double cream and the pie seasoning, maintaining a coarse texture.

Using a plate as a template, cut out two puff pastry discs of 20cm diameter. Place the first disc on a baking tray lined with parchment paper.

Top the pastry disc with the pie mix. Brush the edges with some of the remaining beaten egg and top with the other disc.

Using a fork or your finger, press the pie edges together and trim them. Brush the rest of the beaten egg on the top of the pie.

Bake in the oven until golden brown and cooked in the middle – approx 30 minutes.

To serve, arrange the buttered baby spinach on the plate. Place the pie on top of the spinach and drizzle with chicken jus

Mr White's English Chophouse

Marco Pierre White has teamed-up with New Road Hotel to launch his first ever Chophouse in London. Mr. White's English Chophouse gives a nod to tradition and centres on everything that chophouses are famed for: meat and hearty portions.

The Chophouse menu cleverly combines English classics whilst also introducing a little French flair that epitomizes Marco's cooking style. The menu centres around steaks, grills and chops.

SERVES 1

- 200g lamb rump
- 60g green beans
- 10g butter
- Sea salt
- Black pepper
- 160g dauphinoise potatoes (see page 33)
- 50ml chicken jus
- 15g finely chopped chives
- 10g Dijon mustard
- Olive oil

To serve
- Dauphinoise potatoes
- Green beans, blanched and buttered

Preheat oven to 180C

Season the lamb rump with sea salt and black pepper. In a pan with olive oil, seal the lamb until lightly browned.

Transfer the lamb to a baking tray and roast for 20-25 minutes. Allow the lamb to rest for 5 minutes – lamb will be served pink.

Brush the lamb with Dijon mustard.

To serve, cut the lamb in half and top with chives.

Arrange the blanched green beans on a plate and top with the lamb and warmed dauphinoise potatoes.

Blixen

Cajun spiced monkfish, truffled couscous risotto, kale & red salsa

Blixen is located on the edge of the bustling and vibrant Old Spitalfields Market – a restaurant with its own peaceful atmosphere and vibe. Filled with plants and natural light aplenty, Blixen is an unexpected escape from the buzz of the city.

With a focus on casual European dining and beautiful design, we practise the true spirit of hospitality – arrive happy, leave happier.

We are open seven days a week, offering brunch, lunch and dinner, complemented by an eclectic wine list and exceptional cocktails – both upstairs and at Bar Three, our subterranean cocktail lounge.

SERVES 4

- *4 × 110g monkfish fillet*
- *400g Israeli couscous*
- *100g double cream*
- *160g grated parmesan*
- *20g truffle paste*
- *2 diced plum tomatoes*
- *1 diced shallot*
- *⅓ bunch of chives, chopped*
- *160g purple kale*
- *15g coriander cress*
- *Cajun spice*
- *Vegetable stock*
- *Olive oil*
- *Vegetable oil*

Start by marinating the monkfish with some Cajun spice and vegetable oil. Mix together thoroughly and keep in the fridge for at least two hours.

In a large saucepan cook the couscous in seasoned boiling water for 6 minutes then cool it down in iced water, drain and keep aside.

Make the tomato salsa using the tomatoes, shallots and chives. Mix the ingredients all together with some olive oil, Cajun spice and salt.

When ready to eat cook the fish in a frying pan with some vegetable oil. Whilst cooking, reheat the couscous in a saucepan with the cream and one ladle of vegetable stock. Once boiling, add the parmesan and truffle paste. Adjust consistency with a bit more of vegetable stock if needed and check the seasoning.

For the plating, slice the fish and cook the kale in a pot of seasoned boiling water for 2 minutes.

Spoon the risotto to the bottom of a serving bowl, top with the sliced fish and add the kale all around the plate. Finish with tomato salsa and some coriander cress.

Perfect drink match:
Glass of crisp Portuguese Alvarinho

This outstanding restaurant has pretty much been super popular from the day it opened. The vibe is fusion – Japanese and Italian and it works beautifully. An amazing range of wine and impeccable service mean that Angelina should continue to be a stalwart of culinary innovation for many more years to come.

- *For any 100g of risotto (2 small portions)*
- *300ml of dashi*
- *20g of butter+ 20g more*
- *1 shallot*
- *20ml white wine*
- *10g soy sauce*
- *50 g of unagi*

Chef's tip: put the unagi skin in the dashi for extra flavour

For the dashi:

Bring water to the boil with kelp, add bonito and let infuse for 1 hour

(For each litre of water add 40g of kelp and 40g of bonito)

For the risotto:

Cook small diced shallots with the butter until the shallots start to turn golden in colour

Add the risotto to the shallots and toast for a couple of minutes

Add a splash of white wine and once evaporated begin to add the dashi one cup at a time, continuing to add once absorbed (around 18 to 20 minutes)

Burnt soy butter:

Cook the butter until golden brown with a dash of soy sauce

Finish the risotto with the chopped unagi and burnt soy butter

Imbibe to survive
Cocktails

~~~~~~~~~

Looking Glass Cocktail Club
Butter-Washed Negroni

Looking Glass Cocktail Club
Good Juju

Looking Glass Cocktail Club
Guiness Old Fashioned

MAP Maison
Into the Woods

MAP Maison
Kanji in the Evening

Poptata, the Bar
Mi Hermosita

Dirty Bones
Mutt's Nuts

The vibe is unique in this high-end speakeasy meets illegal warehouse party. The 16th century baroque furniture and distressed oak panelling combine with concrete floors and a rough-and-ready cast-iron bar. Music is house and the dress code relax – trainers are welcome here.

The venue is almost a decade old and was created from the remains of a warehouse used to store car parts. More recently, it housed a record store and then a hair salon before being transformed into a cocktail club it is today. Beginning with the most basic of fit-out and furnishings in its early days, people wondered if it was a pop-up bar, but in actuality the owner took the time to invest their own money – and all these years later, Looking Glass Cocktail Club is a firm fixture on the Shoreditch bar scene.

MAKES 10 – CAN BE STORED

- *250ml Campari*
- *250ml sweet vermouth (choose your favourite)*
- *250ml gin*
- *250g ghee*
- *1 orange*
- *An empty 1.5L plastic bottle*

....

Add the Campari, the sweet vermouth and the gin together in the empty plastic bottle. Set aside.

In a saucepan add the ghee and allow it to melt on a low heat until completely dissolved.

Using a funnel, add the ghee to the bottle. Using the lid, close the bottle, shake it hard for 3 minutes.

Put the bottle upside down in the freezer for 1 hour. This will allow the ghee to solidify again. The remaining liquid forms the Negroni with an amazing buttery taste.

To serve: take heavy-based old fashioned glass. Add a large clear cube of ice. Pour in 70ml of the Negroni infusion and stir. Garnish with an orange peel and a sprig of rosemary. .

Note You can bottle your Negroni and use whenever you want.

Perfect food match:
Aged steak with spicy puree or seasonal roasted vegetables with peppers and aubergine.

Looking Glass Cocktail Club

The vibe is unique in this high-end speakeasy meets illegal warehouse party. The 16th century baroque furniture and distressed oak panelling combine with concrete floors and a rough-and-ready cast-iron bar. Music is house and the dress code relax – trainers are welcome here.

The venue is almost a decade old and was created from the remains of a warehouse used to store car parts. More recently, it housed a record store and then a hair salon before being transformed into a cocktail club it is today. Beginning with the most basic of fit-out and furnishings in its early days, people wondered if it was a pop-up bar, but in actuality the owner took the time to invest their own money – and all these years later, Looking Glass Cocktail Club is a firm fixture on the Shoreditch bar scene.

MAKES 1 COCKTAIL

- *50ml coconut rum*
- *330ml Guinness*
- *500g caster sugar*
- *100g unsalted peanuts*
- *3 small cinnamon sticks*
- *3 star anise*
- *25ml fresh lime juice*

....

For the Guiness syrup: Take a saucepan and pour in the Guinness. Bring the Guiness to 80C (or just before boiling point if you dont have a thermometer)

Add sugar, peanuts, cinnamon and star anise. Stir it until the sugar dissolves completely. Leave the infusion on a very low heat for for 15 min. Remove from the heat and let the liquid cool before straining it with cheese cloth.

In a metal julep cup, add the coconut rum, lime juice, and 20ml of the Guiness syrup. Add some crushed ice and stir for 20 seconds.

Top with more crushed ice and garnish with a cinnamon stick and some fresh thyme.

Note: You can bottle the syrup and use for other cocktails like the Guiness Old Fashioned on page 55. Or use it as a steak sauce or to baste a joint of roast beef.

Perfect food match:
Coconut rum chicken curry

The vibe is unique in this high-end speakeasy meets illegal warehouse party. The 16th century baroque furniture and distressed oak panelling combine with concrete floors and a rough-and-ready cast-iron bar. Music is house and the dress code relax – trainers are welcome here.

The venue is almost a decade old and was created from the remains of a warehouse used to store car parts. More recently, it housed a record store and then a hair salon before being transformed into a cocktail club it is today. Beginning with the most basic of fit-out and furnishings in its early days, people wondered if it was a pop-up bar, but in actuality the owner took the time to invest their own money – and all these years later, Looking Glass Cocktail Club is a firm fixture on the Shoreditch bar scene.

MAKES 1 COCKTAIL

- *50ml whiskey*
- *3 dashes Angostura bitters*
- *5ml Guinness syrup*

....

Take a heavy-based old fashioned glass and add a large clear ice cube (see below instructions on how to make).

Add whiskey, the bitters and Guiness syrup. Stir and garnish with an orange peel.

Instructions on how to make clear ice cubes using directional freezing.

This method is a way of making crystal clear ice cubes in your own freezer. The materials you use, will mean that the freezing process comes from the top only which pushes tiny air bubbles down – it's the tiny air bubbles that make ice look cloudy.

To make large cubes, you'll need a silicon ice tray – these can be purchased from kitchen and homeware stores. Use a pair of scissors or a knife to create holes in the base of each ice cube mould – they should be the width of a chopstick.

Take a small portable ice box (esky or chilly bin) that will fit into the freezer and that is big enough to fit the ice cube tray. Place something durable like a small upturned bowl in the base of the ice box. Place the punctured ice tray on tap. Fill with water to the rim of the ice tray.

Freeze for at least 24 hours before letting the ice box thaw for a few minutes before lifting out the ice cube tray. The holes allow any small air bubles to be pushed downwards through to the base of the ice tray.

MAP Maison a home away from home! They offer something different here: a chic tapas and afternoon tea spot during the day and a buzzing cocktail bar from early evening until late. At weekends come for brunch and on most days guests can book in for experiences such as masterclasses. The menu is seasonal with exceptional cocktails and one of the largest selections of Japanese whiskey and other premium spirits.

MAP Maison takes inspiration from all over the world and brings together a mix of meticulously crafted cocktails. The interior design is a patchwork of beautiful tiles, dark wooden cabinets, exposed brick and rose copper fixtures.

At their online shop, a selection of refined bottled cocktails and gift vouchers are available.

MAKES 1 COCKTAIL

- *50ml Wood's Old Navy Rum*
- *5ml Crème de Mure*
- *1-2ml whiskey barrel bitters*
- *5ml vanilla chai liqueur*
- *Cherry oak wood*

Smoke the mixing glass with cherry oak wood. Do this by using a blow torch on the wood, and then placing on a plate with the glass upturned to catpure the smoke. Burning thyme or rosemary in the same way will give a similar effect.

Next, pour all ingredients into a cocktail mixing glass. Add ice cubes. Stir and fine strain into coupette glass.

Note: Into the Woods is also available as a bottled cocktail from MAP Maison.

Perfect food match:
Slices of Iberico ham or smoked and marinated artichoke or aubergine.

MAP Maison a home away from home! They offer something different here: a chic tapas and afternoon tea spot during the day and a buzzing cocktail bar from early evening until late. At weekends come for brunch and on most days guests can book in for experiences such as masterclasses. The menu is seasonal with exceptional cocktails and one of the largest selections of Japanese whiskey and other premium spirits.

MAP Maison takes inspiration from all over the world and brings together a mix of meticulously crafted cocktails. The interior design is a patchwork of beautiful tiles, dark wooden cabinets, exposed brick and rose copper fixtures.

At their online shop, a selection of refined bottled cocktails and gift vouchers are available.

MAKES 1 COCKTAIL

- *40ml Hakushu Distillers Reserve*
- *10ml blood orange*
- *10ml yellow Chartreuse*
- *20ml homemade pink peppercorn sugar*
- *Smoke with cherry oak wood*

....

Pour all ingredients in to a cocktail shaker. Shake for 30 seconds. Fine strain into an old fashioned glass. Place the glass into glass cake dome and smoke with cherry oak wood.

Poptata, the Bar

Setting up amidst the hustle and bustle of the other colourful food stalls, Marco and Luca (the minds behind Poptata) looked at each other and smiled, sensing that their idea really was going to fill an exciting niche.

It was the height of London's casual dining revolution, and the pair had the brainwave to forge a brilliantly simple new strand within an emerging street food scene – a space that was opening up genuinely good food-on-the-go to foodies bored with the rigidity of traditional restaurants.

MAKES 1

- *30ml Patrón Silver*
- *20ml Aperol Bitter*
- *15ml fresh lime juice*
- *10ml agave syrup*
- *60ml blood orange soda*

Chill the mixing glass, filling it up to ¾ with ice cube (if you don't have a mixing glass you can use a pint glass instead or any container... be creative!

Rub a lime wedge on half rim of a highball glass and dip it into some fine salt, in order to have a nice half-salted rim.

Now it's time to pour the ingredients: Drain the water out of mixing glass, then add the tequila, Aperol, lime juice and agave syrup. Stir for roughly 10 seconds.

Fill up the highball glass with ice cubes and pour the chilled drink into it.

Top up with blood orange soda and garnish with orange wedge.

Dirty Bones is all about the good vibes and high fives – Add a generous dose of NYC-inspired food and drink plus a seriously good soundtrack that people want to listen to while they eat, and you have the ultimate venue in which to drink and play.

Housed in an iconic Grade II-listed heritage building on Club Row, Dirty Bones' history-steeped restaurant and cocktail bar was once home to 1960's pub and institution Knave of Clubs, and they've kept the party alive today. I love Dirty Bones as the perfect post-work cocktail hang out, late-night drinking den or for dinner with friends. Signature dishes include NYC-inspired comfort food classics such as Chicken & Waffles, Flat Iron Steak and Cheeseburger Dumplings.

MAKES 1

- *50ml Woodford Reserve*
- *30ml apple juice*
- *25ml maple syrup*
- *25ml lemon juice*
- *3 dashes Angostura Bitters*
- *An orange for garnish*

....

Add all ingredients to a cocktail shaker and shake vigorously with ice.

Fill an old fashioned glass with ice cubes.

Strain the shaken liquid into the glass.

To garnish, hold the orange in the palm of your hand with a firm grip. Use a paring knife to cut into the orange peel – digging just deep enough to avoid the white pith.

With a smooth, even motion, roll the orange around in your hand, continuing to cut a strip of the peel with the knife as you go. Stop when you have the desired length or until the peel naturally cuts off. Neaten up any rough edges by trimming the sides.

Twist the strip of peel into a spiral. Form as tight a spiral as you can without breaking the peel and give it a gentle squeeze.

Place peel in the top of the glass to serve

Kick back and enjoy!

Perfect food match:
Cheeseburger dumplings.

Ingram Content Group UK Ltd.
Milton Keynes UK
UKHW050317080723
424737UK00002B/19